YOU ALREADY KNOW FRENCH WITHOUT LEARNING ANYTHING:

OVER 1000 WORDS THAT ARE THE SAME IN FRENCH AND ENGLISH:

LEARNING FRENCH THROUGH ENGLISH

CATHERINE-CHANTAL MARANGO

CATHERINE-CHANTAL MARANGO

YOU ALREADY KNOW FRENCH WITHOUT LEARNING ANYTHING: OVER 1000 WORDS THAT ARE THE SAME IN FRENCH AND IN ENGLISH: LEARNING FRENCH THROUGH ENGLISH

YOU ALREADY KNOW FRENCH

WITHOUT LEARNING ANYTHING:

OVER 1000 WORDS THAT ARE THE SAME

IN FRENCH AND ENGLISH:

LEARN FRENCH THROUGH ENGLISH

CATHERINE-CHANTAL MARANGO

YOU ALREADY KNOW FRENCH WITHOUT LEARNING ANYTHING: OVER 1000 WORDS THAT ARE THE SAME IN FRENCH AND IN ENGLISH: LEARNING FRENCH THROUGH ENGLISH

ISBN: 9798611107799

CATHERINE-CHANTAL MARANGO

YOU ALREADY KNOW FRENCH WITHOUT LEARNING ANYTHING: OVER 1000 WORDS THAT ARE THE SAME IN FRENCH AND IN ENGLISH: LEARNING FRENCH THROUGH ENGLISH

DEDICATION

To my all international family, friends, learners and readers
CATHERINE-CHANTAL MARANGO

CONTENTS

YOU ALREADY KNOW FRENCH WITHOUT LEARNING ANYTHING: OVER 1000 WORDS THAT ARE THE SAME IN FRENCH AND IN ENGLISH: LEARNING FRENCH THROUGH ENGLISH

YOU ALREADY KNOW FRENCH WITHOUT LEARNING ANYTHING: OVER 1000 WORDS THAT ARE THE SAME IN FRENCH AND IN ENGLISH: LEARNING FRENCH THROUGH ENGLISH

ACKNOWLEDGMENTS

This book is for my international family, friends, learners and readers
Who always have been major sources of happiness for me
in the compilation of this book and my career

Chapter 1 - French and English nouns that are the same

a) French and English Masculine Nouns ending in « act»

1. Artefact
2. Contact
3. Impact
4. Tact
5. Tract

The rule for the Masculine Noun agreement is the following:

French Masculine nouns that end in "act" follow the same

pattern as in English:

French Masculine singular	French+ English Masculine plural
Artefact	Artefacts
Contact	Contacts
Impact	Impacts
Tact	Tacts
Tract	Tracts

Like in English, French Masculine nouns are converted from singular to plural by adding the -s.

In French, pronunciation remains the same for the   Masculine singular and plural noun, as the plural "S" is silent.

Exercize 1 :

Complete the sentences using the following words in French :

artefacts, contacts, impact, tact et tract

1.   Elle a des………….. au gouvernement
2.   Il manque de ………..
3.   Les manifestants distribuent des ……..
4.   A Strasbourg, le festival des ………. Est un festival de musique
5.   Le ministre de la culture a décidé de d'évaluer …….   que peuvent avoir les projets de lois et de textes réglementaires sur la jeunesse.

b) French and English Feminine and Masculine Nouns ending in « ade»

YOU ALREADY KNOW FRENCH WITHOUT LEARNING ANYTHING: OVER
1000 WORDS THAT ARE THE SAME IN FRENCH AND IN ENGLISH: LEARNING
FRENCH THROUGH ENGLISH

French   English

1. Accolade
2. Arcade
3. Ballade
4. Balustrade
5. Barricade
6. Brigade
7. Cascade
8. Centigrade
9. Charade
10. Chiffonnade
11. Dégringolade   Degringolade
12. Escapade
13. Escalade
14. Façade   Facade
15. Fusillade
16. Galopade
17. Grenade
18. Grillade
19. Marinade
20. Orangeade
21. Parade
22. Promenade
23. Stade
24. Tapenade
25. Tirade

The rule for the Feminine and Masculine noun agreement is the following
one:

French Feminine + Masculine nouns that end in "ade" follow the same
pattern as in English:

French Feminine +Masculine singular	French Feminine plural	English +Masculine
Arcade (F)	Arcades	
Brigade (F)	Brigades	
Grillade (F)	Grillades	
Promenade (F)	Promenades	
Stade (M)	Stades	

Like in English, French and Feminine Masculine nouns are converted from singular to plural by adding the -s

In French, pronunciation remains the same for the Feminine and Masculine singular and plural noun, as the plural "S" is silent.

Complete the sentences using the following words in French :

Promenade, grillades, fusillade, tapenade, orangeade

1. A Nice, la …………… des anglais est célèbre
2. En été, on fait des……. Au barbecue
3. La………… est une spécialité provençale
4. Il y a eu de nombreuses victimes dans cette …………..
5. Boire une ……………… est désaltérant

c) French and English Feminine and Masculine Nouns ending in « age»

French	English
Adage	
Age	
Assemblage	
Badinage	
Bandage	
Barrage	
Brassage	
Bricolage	
Camouflage	
Cartilage	
Chantage	
Colportage	
Coopérage	Cooperage
Corsage	
Courage	
Drainage	
Entourage	
Equipage	
Gage	
Grillage	
Image	
Libertinage	
Manufacturage	
Maquillage	
Message	
Mirage	
Moulage	
Page	
Patronage	
Personnage	
Pillage	
Pilotage	
Plumage	
Rage	
Reportage	
Repassage	
Routage	
Sabotage	
Suffrage	

Vagabondage
Vernissage
Visage
Voltage
Voyage

The rule for the Feminine and Masculine noun
agreement is the following one:
French Feminine +Masculine nouns that end in "age"
 follow the same pattern as in English:

English+French
Feminine   and   Masculine   English+French   Masculine
singular   plural

Age (M)   Ages
Image (F)   Images
Message (M)   Messages
Rage (F)   Rages
Voyage (M)   Voyages

Like in English, French and Feminine Masculine nouns
 are converted from singular to plural by adding the -s.

In French, pronunciation remains the same for the Feminine and
Masculine singular and plural noun, as the plural "S" is silent.

Exercize 3

<u>Complete the sentences using the following words in French:</u>

Age, voyages, image, message, pages

1. Ce livre a 300 ....
2. Il y a un .... Sur le répondeur
3. il aime les....................à l'étranger
4. quel est son ...... ? il est centenaire
5. Un gif est une .... animée

d) French and English Masculine Nouns suffixed with « Arium and Orium»

French   English

1. Aquarium
2. Auditorium
3. Crematorium
4. Planétarium   Planetarium
5. Solarium

The rule for the Masculine noun agreement is the following:

French Masculine nouns that end in "ide" follow the same

pattern as in English:

French Masculine Singular	French Masculine plural +English
Aquarium	Aquariums
Auditorium	Auditoriums
Crématorium	Crematoriums
Planétarium	Planetariums
Solarium	Solariums

Like in English, French Masculine nouns are converted from singular

to plural by adding the -s

In French, pronunciation remains the same for the Masculine singular and plural noun, as the plural "S" is silent.

Exercize 4

<u>Complete the sentences using the following words in French :</u>

Aquarium, auditorium, crématorium, planetarium, solarium

1.   Dans son …………, il y a des poissons exotiques
2.   Le………… est au dernier étage de l'hôtel
Le …………. permet de découvrir
les phénomènes célestes de l'univers
3.   ……………… accueille plus de 1000 places
assises et reçoit chaque saison une cinquantaine de concerts
4.   Le ……………… est un équipement de la ville
de Paris

e) French and English Nouns ending in « cide»

French   English

1. Bactéricide
2. Génocide
3. Herbicide
4. Homicide
5. Infanticide
6. Insecticide
7. Parricide
8. Pesticide
9. Spermicide
10. Suicide

The rule for the Masculine noun agreement is the following one:

French Masculine nouns that end in "ide" follow the same pattern as in English:

French Masculine singular	French +English Masculine plural

Bactéricide	Bactericides
Génocide	Génocides
Homicide	Homicides
Insecticide	Insecticides
Pesticide	Pesticides

Like in English, French Masculine nouns are converted from singular to plural by adding the -s

In French, pronunciation remains the same for the Masculine singular and plural noun, as the plural "S" is silent.

Exercize 5

<u>Complete the sentences using the following words in French :</u>

Pesticides, génocide, homicide, insecticides, bactéricide

1. Il a trop de ……….. dans les fruits et légumes
2. Il y a eu trois morts dans un ………… par balle
3. Le ……….. arménien a été reconnu
4. Il y a des …………. Naturels contre les poux
5. Un…… est un antimicrobien

YOU ALREADY KNOW FRENCH WITHOUT LEARNING ANYTHING: OVER
1000 WORDS THAT ARE THE SAME IN FRENCH AND IN ENGLISH: LEARNING
FRENCH THROUGH ENGLISH

24

f) French and English Nouns ending in « ence»

French   English

1. Absence
2. Abstinence
3. Adhérence
4. Adolescence
5. Affluence
6. Audience
7. Cadence
8. Coexistence
9. Cohérence   Coherence
10. Compétence   Competence
11. Concurrence
12. Confidence
13. Conséquence   Consequence
14. Convalescence
15. Convergence
16. Continence
17. Déférence   Deference
18. Diligence
19. Essence
20. Evidence
21. Existence
22. Flatulence
23. Impertinence
24. Indifférence   Indifference
25. Influence
26. Insolence
27. Intelligence
28. Interférence   Interference
29. Jurisprudence
30. Magnificence
31. Négligence   Negligence
32. Occurrence
33. Omnipotence
34. Opalescence
35. Pénitence   Penitence
36. Permanence
37. Prudence

38. Quintessence
39. Référence   Reference
40. Réminiscence   Reminiscence
41. Résidence   Residence
42. Reticence
43. Révérence   Reverence
44. Science
45. Sentence
46. Séquence   Sequence
47. Silence
48. Somnolence
49. Turbulence
50. Violence
51. Virulence

The rule for the Feminine noun agreement is the f:ollowing one

French Feminine and Masculine nouns that end in "ence" follow the same pattern as in English:

French Feminine singular	French+English Feminine plural
Absence (F)	Absences
Intelligence(F)	Intelligences
Science (F)	Sciences
Silence (M)	Silences
Violence (F)	Violences

Like in English, French Feminine and Masculine nouns

are converted from singular to plural by adding the -s

In French, pronunciation remains the same for the

 Masculine singular and plural noun, as the plural "S" is silent.

Exercize 6

<u>Complete the sentences using the following words in French :</u>

Absences, intelligence, sciences, violence, silence

1. Il est bon en ……….
2. Il est doté d'une grande ………
3. La………. conjugale est un crime
4. Le ……. la nuit est agréable
5. Les…………. répétées des salariés s'appellent l'absentéisme

g) French and English Feminine and Masculine Nouns ending in « ile»
1. Bibliophile
2. Automobile
3. Bile
4. Crocodile
5. Domicile
6. Missile
7. Pile
8. Reptile
9. Textile

YOU ALREADY KNOW FRENCH WITHOUT LEARNING ANYTHING: OVER 1000 WORDS THAT ARE THE SAME IN FRENCH AND IN ENGLISH: LEARNING FRENCH THROUGH ENGLISH

The rule for the Feminine noun agreement is the following one :

French Feminine and Masculine nouns that end in l'ile" follow the same pattern as in English:

French Feminine and Masculine singular	French +English Feminine and Masculine plural
Automobile (F)	Automobiles
Crocodile (M)	Crocodiles
Domicile (F)	Domiciles
Reptile (M)	Reptiles
Textile (F)	Textiles

Like in English, French Feminine and Masculine nouns are

Converted from singular to plural by adding the -s

In French, pronunciation remains the same for the Masculine singular and plural noun, as the plural "S" is silent.

Exercize 7

<u>Complete the sentences using the following words in French :</u>

Automobile, domicile, reptiles, missile, piles

1.C'est le salon de l'.............. à Monaco
2.Un sans .... fixe n'a pas de maison
3.Il y a beaucoup de .... En Australie

4.Mon téléphone ne marche plus, les .... sont mortes
5.Les frappes aériennes ont lancé un ....

h) *French and English Feminine Nouns ending in « ion »*

French   English

1. Abdication
2. Abnégation   Abnegation
3. Aberration
4. Abomination
5. Abrogation
6. Absolution
7. Absorption
8. Abstention
9. Abstraction
10. Accentuation
11. Accumulation
12. Accusation
13. Addiction
14. Administration
15. Acquisition
16. Admiration
17. Admission
18. Abnégation   Abnegation
19. Abstraction
20. Acculturation
21. Accusation
22. Acquisition
23. Action
24. Adaptation
25. Administration
26. Admission
27. Admiration

28. Adoration
29. Affectation
30. Affection
31. Agglomération   Agglomeration
32. Altercation
33. Aspiration
34. Assertion
35. Agitation
36. Allusion
37. Ambition
38. Amplification
39. Amputation
40. Animation
41. Annihilation
42. Annotation
43. Anticipation
44. Apparition
45. Application
46. Appropriation
47. Approximation
48. Attraction
49. Ascension
50. Aspiration
51. Assertion
52. Assimilation
53. Association
54. Attention
55. Attraction
56. Attribution
57. Augmentation
58. Automation
59. Aversion
60. Aviation
61. Calcification
62. Capitulation
63. Castration
64. Caution
65. Certification
66. Cession
67. Circulation

68. Clarification
69. Classification
70. Coagulation
71. Coalition
72. Cognition
73. Cohésion
74. Collaboration
75. Collation
76. Collection
77. Collision
78. Collusion
79. Coloration
80. Combustion
81. Commission
82. Compensation
83. Composition
84. Complication
85. Concession
86. Compression
87. Concentration
88. Conciliation
89. Conclusion
90. Conception
91. Condensation
92. Condition
93. Confession
94. Configuration
95. Confirmation
96. Confrontation
97. Confusion
98. Connotation
99. Contagion
100. Contamination
101. Continuation
102. Correction
103. Conservation
104. Consolation
105. Consolidation
106. Continuation
107. Contraception

108. Contradiction
109. Contribution
110. Conversation
111. Conviction
112. Coordination
113. Corruption
114. Déclaration   Declaration

115. Dépréciation   Depreciation
116. Dérision   Derision
117. Description
118. Destination
119. Destitution
120. Destruction
121. Diffusion
122. Digestion
123. Dimension
124. Diminution
125. Direction
126. Discrimination
127. Discussion
128. Dispensation
129. Dissension
130. Dissolution
131. Diversion
132. Documentation
133. Domestication
134. Domination
135. Donation
136. Duplication
137. Education
138. Election
139. Elévation   Elevation
140. Emotion
141. Erosion
142. Estimation
143. Eviction
144. Exaltation
145. Exception
146. Exclusion

147. Excursion
148. Exécration   Execration
149. Exhibition
150. Expansion
151. Expiration
152. Exploitation
153. Exploration
154. Explosion
155. Exportation
156. Exposition
157. Expression
158. Expulsion
159. Extermination
160. Extinction
161. Extraction
162. Extradition
163. Expansion
164. Expulsion
165. Formation
166. Gesticulation
167. Glorification
168. Gradation
169. Graduation
170. Gravitation
171. Habitation
172. Hallucination
173. Hibernation
174. Identification
175. Illumination
176. Illusion
177. Illustration
178. Imagination
179. Illustration
180. Imagination
181. Imitation
182. Immigration
183. Impression
184. Improvision
185. Improvisation
186. Incorporation

187. Incrimination
188. Incubation
189. Indication
190. Indigestion
191. Inflammation
192. Inflation
193. Infusion
194. Inscription
195. Inspiration
196. Installation
197. Institution
198. Instruction
199. Insurrection
200. Interrogation
201. Interruption
202. Intersection
203. Intervention
204. Intimidation
205. Intoxication
206. Introduction
207. Introspection
208. Introversion
209. Intuition
210. Invasion
211. Invention
212. Inversion
213. Investigation
214. Involution
215. Irritation
216. Isolation
217. Jubilation
218. Justification
219. Juxtaposition
220. Lamentation
221. Libération   Liberation
222. Limitation
223. Lion
224. Liquidation
225. Location
226. Machination

227. Malnutrition
228. Manifestation
229. Maturation
230. Menstruation
231. Mention
232. Million
233. Mission
234. Modification
235. Modulation
236. Multiplication
237. Mystification
238. Narration
239. Nation
240. Navigation
241. Nomination
242. Notification
243. Objection
244. Obligation
245. Observation
246. Obsession
247. Obstruction
248. Occasion
249. Occlusion
250. Occupation
251. Omission
252. Opinion
253. Opposition
254. Oppression
255. Orientation
256. Ovulation
257. Palpitation
258. Participation
259. Passion
260. Pension
261. Perception
262. Percussion
263. Perfection
264. Perforation
265. Persuasion
266. Perturbation

267. Perversion
268. Plantation
269. Pollution
270. Population
271. Possession
272. Précision   Precision
273. Prescription
274. Profession
275. Promotion
276. Propagation
277. Proportion
278. Prostitution
279. Protection
280. Protestation
281. Provision
282. Portion
283. Publication
284. Purification
285. Qualification
286. Radiation
287. Ratification
288. Reconstitution
289. Reconstruction
290. Réduction   Reduction
291. Région   Region
292. Régression   Regression
293. Régulation   Regulation
294. Relation
295. Religion
296. Reproduction
297. Révolution   Revolution
298. Réservation   Reservation
299. Résiliation   Resiliation
300. Respiration
301. Restriction
302. Rotation
303. Salutation
304. Satisfaction
305. Saturation
306. Sécrétion   Secretion

307. Séparation   Separation
308. Simplification
309. Sophistication
310. Station
311. Submersion
312. Subordination
313. Substitution
314. Subvention
315. Succession
316. Suffocation
317. Suggestion
318. Superstition
319. Supervision
320. Suspension
321. Suspicion
322. Tabulation
323. Taxation
323. Télévision   Television
324. Tension
325. Torsion
326. Traction
327. Tradition
328. Traduction
329. Transaction
330. Transcription
331. Transformation
332. Transfusion
333. Transgression
334. Transition
335. Transmission
336. Union
337. Usurpation
338. Vaccination
339. Vacation
340. Validation
341. Variation
342. Ventilation
343. Vibration
344. Vision
345. Vivisection

346. Vocation

The rule for the Feminine noun agreement is the following one:

French Feminine nouns that end in "ion" follow

the same pattern as in English:

French Feminine singular	French Feminine plural +English
Correction	Corrections
Emotion	Emotions
Opinion	Opinions
Simplification	Simplifications
Vocation	Vocations

Like in English, French feminine nouns are converted
from singular to plural
by adding the -s
In French, pronunciation remains the same for the
Feminine singular and plural noun, as the plural "S" is
silent.

Exercize 8

Complete the sentences using the following words in French :

Formation, location, relations, tradition, vocation

Complete the sentences using the following words in French :

Formation, location, relations, tradition, vocation

1. Les ………….. internationales sont complexes
2. J'ai trois biens immobiliers en ……………..
3. C'est une …………… de manger la bûche à Noël, en France
4. Il suit une …………. en droit
5. La ………… de Rodin était de devenir le père de la sculpture moderne

i. French and English Feminine Nouns ending in « Ne»

French

English

1. Adénosine — adenosine
2. Adrénaline — adrenaline
3. Amphétamine — amphetamine
4. Aubergine
5. Caféine — afeine
6. Canine
7. Chaîne — chaine
8. Chine
9. Cocaïne — cocaine
10. Codéine — codeine
11. Cuisine
12. Discipline
13. Doctrine
14. Dopamine
15. Famine
16. Figurine
17. Gamine
18. Guillotine

19. Héroïne
20. Hotline
21. Langoustine
22. Limousine
23. Machine
24. Margarine
25. Morphine
26. Mousseline
27. Narine
28. Nectarine
29. Nicotine
30. Piscine
31. Praline
32. Routine
33. Sardine
34. Seine
35. Toxine
36. Urine
37. Vitamine
38. Vitrine

The rule for the Feminine noun agreement is the following one. French Feminine nouns that end in "ne" follow the same pattern as in English:

French Feminine singular	French +English Feminine plural
Aubergine	Aubergines
Cuisine	Cuisines

Piscine	Piscines
Routine	Routines
Vitamine	Vitamines

Like in English, French feminine nouns are converted from singular to plural by adding the -s.

In French, pronunciation remains the same for the Feminine singular and plural noun as the plural "S" is silent.

Exercize 8

Complete the sentences using the following words in French :

Vitamines, cuisine, piscine, routine, vitrines

1. Les ………… de Noël sont bien décorées à Paris
2. Les………….. sont bonnes pour la santé
3. La …………… française est un art
4. Nager à la …………. est agréable
5. La ………… peut être ennuyeuse

j. French and English Masculine Nouns ending in « ple»

1. Couple
2. Disciple
3. Centuple
4. Quadruple
5. Quintuple
6. Temple
7. Triple

The rule for the Masculine noun agreement is the following on

French Feminine nouns that end in "Ple" follow the same pattern as

in English:

French and English Masculine singular	French +English Masculine plural
Couple	Couples
Disciple	Disciples
Temple	Temples

Like in English, French Masculine nouns are converted from singular to plural by adding the -s

Exercize 9

<u>Complete the sentences using the following words in French :</u>

Couple, temple, triple

1. Neuf est le ……. De trois
2. Le Parthénon à Athènes est un ……..grec
3. Ils forment un très joli couple

K .French and English Nouns ending in « ude»

French   English

1. Altitude
2. Amplitude
3. Aptitude
4. Attitude
5. Béatitude   Beatitude
6. Certitude
7. Désuétude   Desuetude
8. Etude
9. Exactitude
10. Finitude
11. Fortitude
12. Gratitude
13. Habitude
14. Ingratitude
15. Latitude
16. Lassitude
17. Longitude
18. Magnitude
19. Mansuétude
20. Platitude
21. Plénitude
22. Promptitude
23. Quiétude
24. Rectitude
25. Vicissitude
26. Servitude
27. Similitude
28. Solitude

The rule for the Feminine noun agreement is the

following one :

French Feminine nouns that end in "ude" follow the sam

pattern as in English:

French and English Feminine singular	French +English Feminine plural
Altitude	Altitudes
Certitude	Certitudes
Habitude	Habitudes
Similitude	Similtudes
Solitude	Solitudes

Like in English, French feminine nouns are converted

from singular to plural by adding the -s

In French, pronunciation remains the same for the Feminine

singular and plural noun as the plural "S" is silent.

Exercize 11

<u>Complete the sentences using the following words</u>

<u>in French :</u>

Altitude, certitude , études, Habitude, solitude

1. Le mont blanc est à 4800 mètres d'..........
2. Il souffre de ....
3. J'ai la .... d'être heureux
4. J'ai l'.......... de me lever tous les jours à 6
Heures du matin

5.   J'ai fait .... supérieures à la Sorbonne

Chapter 2- French and English adjectives that are the same

a) French and English adjectives ending in « al »

French

1. Abyssal
2. Adjectival
3. Adverbal
4. amoral
5. ancestral
6. astral
7. Auroral
8. Bestial
9. Buccal
10. Cantonal
11. Capital
12. cardinal
13. central
14. Colonial
15. Continental
16. Convivial
17. Discal
18. Editorial
19. Electoral
20. Final
21. Focal
22. Fluvial
23. Génial   Genial
24. Illégal
25. Jovial
26. Hibernal
27. Hormonal
28. Intestinal

29. Labial
30. Létal   Letal
31. Machinal
32. Maximal
33. Mental
34. Minimal
35. Musical
36. Nasal
37. Naval
38. Neural
39. Normal
40. Ogival
41. Orbital
42. Orchestral
43. Pictural
44. Pivotal
45. principal
46. Sociétal   Societal
47. Sculptural
48. Territorial
49. Total
50. Tribal
51. Tubal
52. Tropical
53. Vaginal
54. Vénal   Venal
55. Viral
56. Vital
57. Vocal

YOU ALREADY KNOW FRENCH WITHOUT LEARNING ANYTHING: OVER 1000 WORDS THAT ARE THE SAME IN FRENCH AND IN ENGLISH: LEARNING FRENCH THROUGH ENGLISH

The rule for the adjective agreement in French is the following one :

French adjectives that end in –al follow this pattern:

Masculine S	Fem Sing	Masc PLural	Fem Plural
Ancestral	ancestrale	ancestraux	ancestrales
Capital	capitale	capitaux	capitales
Hibernal	hibernale	hibernaux	hibernales
Intestinal	intestinale	intestinaux	intestinales
Principal	principale	principaux	principales
Radical	radicale	radicaux	radicales
Vital	vitale	vitaux	vitales

French and English Masculine adjectives ending in "al" remain the same for the Masculine singular form.

Masculine singular adjectives end with al change to aux for the masculine plural

Masculine singular adjectives end with al change to ale for the feminine singular

Feminine singular adjectives end with ale change to ales for the feminine plural

Exercize 12

Complete the sentences using the following words in French :

Capital, vitale, normal, géniaux, principale

1. Manger et dormir sont de nécessité ………
2. Il est …………. De travailler
3. Tous les sports sont……..
4. Ma ………. activité de loisir est la chasse
5. il a été puni pour un crime……

b)French and English adjectives ending in « able»

1. Abandonnable
2. Abominable
3. Abusable
4. Accentuable
5. Accusable
6. Accumulable
7. Actionable
8. Adaptable
9. Admirable
10. Adoptable
11. Affable
12. Aidable
13. Aimable
14. Aliénable
15. Altérable
16. Amassable

17. Amplifiable
18. Analysable
19. Applicable
20. Articulable
21. Assemblable
22. Associable
23. Attachable
24. Baptisable
25. Battable
26. Blâmable
27. Calculable
28. Capitalisable
29. Causable
30. Certifiable
31. Charitable
32. Citable
33. Civilisable
34. Clarifiable
35. Colonisable
36. Comparable
37. Composable
38. Condensable
39. Configurable
40. Confirmable
41. Contestable
42. Continuable
43. Copiable
44. Curable
45. Déclinable
46. Décodable
47. Drainable
48. Editable
49. Ejectable
50. Employable
51. Endurable
52. Enviable
53. Equipable
54. Estimable
55. Evaluable
56. Excitable

57. Excusable
58. Exécutable
59. Exonérable
60. Expirable
61. Exploitable
62. Explosible
63. Faxable
64. Fermentable
65. Généralisable
66. Glorifiable
67. Gratifiable
68. Habitable
69. Idéalisable
70. Identifiable
71. Ignorable
72. Imaginable
73. Imitable
74. Impeccable
75. Improbable
76. Implacable
77. Incomparable
78. Inconsolable
79. Indispensable
80. Indubitable
81. Inexcusable
82. Inexplicable
83. Inexorable
84. Infectable
85. Inflammable
86. Inimitable
87. Insatiable
88. Insupportable
89. Interceptable
90. Interchangeable
91. Interminable
92. Intolérable
93. Invariable
94. Irrigable
95. Lamentable
96. Légalisable

97. Localisable
98. Manipulable
99. Modernisable
100. Modifiable
101. Multipliable
102. Navigable
103. Notable
104. Notifiable
105. Observable
106. Opposable
107. Optimisable
108. Payable
109. Personnalisable
110. Personifiable
111. Pliable
112. Potable
113. Portable
114. Préférable
115. Préparable
116. Presentable
117. Probable
118. Programmable
119. Projectable
120. Proposable
121. Purifiable
122. Qualifiable
123. Radicalisable
124. Réalisable
125. Recyclable
126. Rechargeable
127. Rectifiable
128. Récupérable
129. Réformable
130. Refusable
131. Regardable
132. Regrettable
133. Régularisable
134. Remédiable
135. Rentable
136. Respectable

137. Ruinable
138. Segmentable
139. Socialisable
140. Solidifiable
141. Solvable
142. Stable
143. Superposable
144. Supportable
145. Supposable
146. Symbolisable
147. Taxable
148. Tenable
149. Terminable
150. Testable
151. Touchable
152. Universalisable
153. Usurpable
154. Utilisable
155. Variable

French adjectives that end in –able follow this pattern:

Masculine and Feminine French+ English singular	Masculine +Feminine Fr Plural
Admirable	Admirables
Comparable	Comparables
Potable	Potables
Respectable	Respectables
Stable	Stables
Utilisable	Utilisables
Variable	Variables

French and English Masculine adjectives ending in "able" remain the same for the Masculine and Feminine singular form.

Feminine and Masculine singular French adjectives end in "able" change to "ables" for the Masculine and Feminine plural

In French, pronunciation remains the same for the Masculine and Feminine singular and plural adjective as the plural "S" is silent.

Exercize 13

Complete the sentences using the following words in French :

potable, portable, rechargeable, respectable

1. L'eau du robinet est ………..
2. J'utilise toujours mon ordinateur ……..
3. C'est une femme ……….
4. C'est un appareil ……….
5. Il a toujours faim, il est ………….

c. French and English adjectives ending in « act »

1. Compact
2. Exact

3. Inexact
4. Intact
5. Ultracompact

The rules for adjective agreement in French are the following ones :

French and English Masculine adjectives ending in "act" remain the same for the
Masculine singular form.

Masculine plural French adjectives end in "act" change
to "acts" for the Masculine French singular form
Feminine singular French adjectives end in "ac"t
change to "acte" for the Feminine French singular form.
Feminine Plural French adjectives end in "act" change
to "actes" for the Feminine French plural form.
In French, pronunciation remains the same for the Masculine
singular and plural adjectives as the plural "S" is silent.

Exercize 14

<u>Complete the sentences using the following words in French :</u>

Compact, exacte, intact

1. C'est un disque dur de fiable diamètre, il est ……..
2. C'est la vérité……..
3. Le trésor est entier, il est resté …….

d)French and English adjectives ending in « ant »

1. Accélérant
2. Acceptant
3. Arrogant
4. Coagulant
5. Continuant
6. Constant
7. Distant
8. Dénaturant   Denaturant
9. Errant

10. Exorbitant
11. Extravagant
12. Flippant
13. Ignorant
14. Important
15. Incessant
16. Irritant
17. Luxuriant
18. Nonchalant
19. Poignant
20. Protestant
21. Quadrant
22. Radiant
23. Revitalisant
24. Stagnant
25. Stimulant
26. Vibrant

The rules for adjective agreement in French are the following ones:

French adjectives that end in –act follow this pattern:

French and English Masculine adjectives ending in "ant" remain the same for the Masculine singular form.

Masculine plural French adjectives end in ant change to "ants " for the Masculine French singular form

Feminine singular French adjectives end in ant change

to "ante" for the Feminine French singular form.

Feminine Plural French adjectives end in act change to "antes

" for the Feminine French plural form.

Exercize 16

<u>Complete the sentences using the following words in French :</u>

, important, convainquant, stimulant

     1.   C'est un argument…..
     2.   La pollution est un sujet écologique ….
     3.   Le café est …….

e) French and English adjectives ending in « ent »

1. *Absent*
2. *Abstinent*
3. *Adjacent*
4. *Adolescent*
5. *Ambivalent*
6. *Antécédent*
7. *Apparent*
8. *Arborescent*
9. *Ardent*
10. *Astringent*
11. *Cohérent*   *coherent*
12. *Compétent*   *competent*
13. *Concurrent*
14. *Contingent*
15. *Convalescent*
16. *Corpulent*
17. *Diligent*

18. *Différent*   different
19. *Divergent*
20. *Effervescent*
21. *Emergent*
22. *Equivalent*
23. *Evanescent*
24. *Excellent*
25. *Fluorescent*
26. *Imminent*
27. *Impudent*
28. *Impertinent*
29. *Incandescent*
30. *Indigent*
31. *Indulgent*
32. *Innocent*
33. *Insolent*
34. *Intermittent*
35. *Jubilent*
36. *Latent*
37. *Luminescent*
38. *Omnipotent*
39. *Omniprésent*   omnipresent
40. *Opulent*
41. *Phosphorescent*
42. *Récurrent*   recurrent
43. *Somnolent*
44. *Succulent*
45. *Trident*
46. *Turbulent*
47. *Véhément*   vehement
48. *Vigilent*
49. *Violent*
50. *Virulent*

The rules for adjective agreement in French are the following ones :

French adjectives that end in –ent follow this pattern:

Masculine French+ English singular	Feminine French Singular	Masc Fr Plural
Absent	Absente	Absents
Innocent	Innocente	Innocents
Succulent	Succulente	Succulents
Violent	Violente	Violents

French and English Masculine adjectives ending in "ent" remain the same for the Masculine singular form.

Masculine plural French adjectives end in "ent" change to "ents" for the Masculine French singular form

Feminine singular French adjectives end in "ent" change to "ente" for the Feminine French singular form.

Feminine Plural French adjectives end in "ent" change to "entes" for the Feminine French plural form.

In French, pronunciation remains the same for the Masculine singular and plural adjective as the plural "S" is silent.

Exercize 16

Complete the sentences using the following words in French :

Innocent, effervescent, excellent, violent , succulent

1. *Il plaide ………… devant la cour*
2. *C'est un comprimé …….*
3. *C'est un mets …………*
4. *Il est agressif, il a un tempérament ….*
5. *Ses résultats scolaires sont parfaits, il est ……………*

f) French and English adjectives ending in « esque »

1. Arabesque
2. Burlesque
3. Filmesque
4. Grotesque
5. Romanesque
6. Statuesque

The rules for adjective agreement in French

French adjectives that end in – esque   follow this pattern:

Masculine and Feminine   French+   Masculine and English singular

Fem French P

Arabesque   Arabesque

Burlesque	Burlesques
Grotesque	Grotesques
Romanesque	Romanesques
Statuesque	Statuesques

French and English Masculine and Feminine adjectives ending in "que" remain the same for the Masculine and Feminine singular form.

Masculine and Feminine plural French adjectives end in -esque change to "-esques" for the Masculine and Feminine French plural form.

In French, pronunciation remains the same for the Feminine singular and plural noun as the plural "S" is silent.

Exercize 17

<u>Complete the sentences using the following words in French :</u>

Grotesques, romanesque, burlesque, statuesque

1. C'est un personnage bizarre, il est ....
2. Les romans d'amour, policiers, d'autobiographie
3. Sont du genre.........

4. Charlie Chaplin avait un genre.......

5. Cette femme est sculpturale, elle a une beauté ....

g) French and English adjectives ending in « etc »

1. Abject
2. Correct
3. Direct
4. Incorrect
5. Indirect
6. Infect

The rules for adjective agreement in French are the following ones :

French adjectives that end in –ect follow this pattern:

Masculine French+ English singular	Feminine French Singular	Masculine French Plural
Abject	Abjecte	Abjects
Correct	Correcte	Corrects

Direct	Directe	Directs
Infect	Infecte	
		infects

French and English Masculine adjectives ending in "ect" remain the same for the Masculine singular form.

Masculine plural French adjectives end in "ect" change to "ects" for the Masculine French plural form.

Feminine singular French adjectives end in "ect" change to "ecte"for the Feminine French singular form.

Feminine Plural French adjectives end in "ect" change to "ectes"
for the Feminine French plural form.

In French, pronunciation remains the same for the Feminine singular and plural noun as the plural "S" is silent.

Exercize 18

Complete the sentences using the following words in French :

Infecte, correct, direct

1. Cette viande est avariée, elle est …….
2. C'est un complément d'objet ………
3. C'est un garçon poli, il est ……….

68

h) French and English adjectives ending in « ial »

1. Adverbial
2. Bestial
3. Colonial
4. Convivial
5. Cordial
6. Facial
7. Familial
8. Filial
9. Impartial
10. Impérial
11. Jovial
12. Martial
13. Matrimonial
14. Nuptial
15. Primordial
16. Social
17. Spatial
18. Spécial   special
19. Trivial
20. Vicarial

The rules for adjective agreement in French are the following ones :

French adjectives that end in –ial follow this pattern:

Masculine singular	Feminine singular	Masculine plural	Feminine plural
Adverbial	adverbiale	adverbiaux	adverbiales
Bestial	bestiale	bestiaux	bestiales
Colonial	coloniale	coloniaux	coloniales
Cordial	cordiale	cordiaux	cordiales
Familial	familiale	familiaux	familiales
Impartial	impartiale	impartiaux	impartiales
Social	sociale	sociaux	sociales

French and English Masculine adjectives ending in "ial" remain the same for the Masculine singular form.

Masculine singular adjectives end with" ial" change to

"iaux" for the masculine plural

Masculine singular adjectives end in "ial" change to

"iale" for the feminine singular

Feminine singular adjectives end in " iale" change to"

 iales" for the feminine plural

Exercize 19

Complete the sentences using the following words in French :

Cordiale, familiaux, spéciaux, spatiale, social

1.	Cet enfant a des problèmes ....
2.	C'est une navette………
3.	Ce sont des régimes de retraite……….
4.	Notre entente est…………..
5.	La conjoncture…………….n'est pas très bonne

i) French and English adjectives ending in « ible »

1. Accessible
2. Audible
3. Coercible
4. Combustible
5. Compatible
6. Compréhensible
7. Constructible
8. Convertible
9. Conductible
10. Convincible
11. Corruptible
12. Digestible
13. Divisible
14. Flexible
15. Horrible
16. Immersible
17. Imperceptible
18. Impossible
19. Inaccessible
20. Inadmissible
21. Incorrigible

22. Incompatible
23. Indestructible
24. Indivisible
25. Infaillible
26. Inflexible
27. Insensible
28. Irréversible   `irreversible`
29. Intelligible
30. Invincible
31. Irrésistible   `irresistible`
32. Ostensible
33. Perfectible
34. Plausible
35. Perceptible
36. Possible

37. Répréhensible   reprehensible
38. Répressible   repressible
39. Reproductible
40. Résistible   resistible
41. Risible
42. Tangible
43. Transmissible
44. Visible

The rules for adjective agreement in French are the following ones :

French adjectives that end in –ible follow this pattern:

Masculine and Feminine French+ English singular	Masculine +Fem Fr Plural
Accessible	Accessibles
Compatible	Compatibles
Horrible	Horribles
Invincible	Invincibles
Visible	Visibles

French and English Masculine and Feminine adjectives ending in "ble" remain the same for the Masculine and Feminine singular form.

Masculine and Feminine plural French adjectives end in -ble change to "-bles" for the Masculine and Feminine

French plural form.

In French, pronunciation remains the same for the Feminine and Masculine singular and plural adjective as the plural "S" is silent.

Exercize 20

Complete the sentences using the following words in French :

Accessible, compatibles, horrible, invicible, visible

1. C'est un fait divers ……
2. Nice est ………. Par l'autoroute
3. Ces mesures sociales ne sont pas ….
4. C'est le champion du monde d'athlétisme , il est …..
5. Il est …… sur tous les réseaux sociaux

j) French and English adjectives ending in « ient»

1. Déficient   Deficient
2. Efficient
3. Impatient
4. Inconscient
5. Omniscient
6. Patient

The rules for adjective agreement in French

French adjectives that end in –ect follow this pattern:

Masculine French+ English singular	Feminine French Singular	Masculine French Plural	Feminine French Plural
Efficient	Efficiente	Efficients	Abjectes
Impatient	Impatiente	Impatients	Impatientes
Inconscient	Inconsciente	Inconscients	Inconscientes
Patient	Patiente	Patients	Patientes

French and English Masculine adjectives ending in "ect" remain the same for the Masculine singular form.

Masculine plural French adjectives end in "ect" change to "ects" for the Masculine French plural form.

Feminine singular French adjectives end in "ect" change to "ecte" for the Feminine French singular form.

Feminine Plural French adjectives end in "ect" change to "ectes" for the Feminine French plural form.

In French, pronunciation remains the same for the Masculine singular and plural adjective as the plural "S" is silent.

Exercize 21

Complete the sentences using the following words in French
Déficient, impatient, inconscient, efficiente, patient
1.	Il a une anémie, il est …….. en fer
2.	Il sait attendre, il est …..
3.	Il ne supporte pas d'attendre, il est ……
4.	Il est ……. du danger
5.	C'est une méthode qui marche, elle est …..

k) French and English adjectives ending in « ile»

1. Agile
2. Bibliophile
3. Docile
4. Facile
5. Fébrile
6. Fertile
7. Fragile
8. Futile
9. Hostile
10. Imbécile
11. Immobile
12. Juvénile
13. Mercantile
14. Mobile
15. Nubile
16. Puérile
17. Sénile
18. Servile
19. Tactile
20. Textile
21. Versatile
22. Virile
23. Volatile

The rules for adjective agreement in French is the following :

The French adjectives that end in –ile follow this pattern:

Masculine   French+   Masculine + feminine
Feminine English singular   French Plural

Fragile	Fragiles
Hostile	Hostiles
Mobile	Mobiles
Virile	Viriles

French and English Masculine and Feminine adjectives

ending in "ile" remain the same for the singular form.

Masculine and Feminine plural French adjectives end

in "ile" change to "ile" for the Masculine and Masculine French plural form.

Feminine singular French adjectives end in "ect" change

to "ecte" for the Feminine French singular form.

Feminine Plural French adjectives end in "ect" change to

"ectes" for the Feminine French plural form.

In French, pronunciation remains the same for the

Feminine and Masculine singular and plural adjective as

the plural "S" is silent.

Exercize 22

Complete the sentences using the following words in French

Fragile, hostile, mobile, virile, facile

1. Il est toujours malade, il est de santé .....
2. Il est très masculin, il fait ....
3. Le français est une langue.....
4. Ce bureau est ....., il peut être déplacé
5. C'est un individu dangereux, son comportement est...

I.French and English adjectives ending in « ne»

1. Bovine
2. Clandestine
3. Divine
4. Féline
5. Féminine
6. Libertine
7. Masculine
8. Sanguine

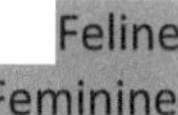

The rules for adjective agreement in French are the following ones

French adjectives that end in –ine follow this pattern

Feminine French+English singular	Feminine French Plural
Clandestine	Clandestines
Divine	Divines
Masculine	Masculines
Sanguine	Sanguines

French and English Feminine adjectives ending in "ine" remain the same for the singular form.

Feminine plural French adjectives end in "ne" change to "nes" for the Feminine French

In French, pronunciation remains the same for the Feminine and Masculine singular and plural adjective as the plural "S" is silent.

Exercize 23

Complete the sentences using the following words in French

plural form.

Clandestine, divine, masculine, sanguines

1. C'est une mesure interdite par la loi, elle est considérée comme......
2. Elle est très belle, sa beauté est.....
3. Il a une allure très ......
4. Ces oranges sont ....

M.French and English adjectives ending in « ple»
1. Ample
2. Multiple
3. Quadruple
4. Quintuple
5. Simple
6. Triple

The rules for adjective agreement in French are the following ones:

French adjectives that end in –ine follow this pattern:

Masculine and Feminine French+English singular	Masculine and Feminine French F
Ample	Amples
Multiple	Multiples
Simple	Simples
Triple	Triples

French and English Masculine and Feminine adjectives ending in "ple" remain the same for the singular form.

Masculine and Feminine plural French adjectives end in "ple" change to "ples" for the Masculine and Feminine French plural form.

In French, pronunciation remains the same for the Masculine and Feminine singular and plural adjective as the plural "S" is silent.

Exercize 24

Complete the sentences using the following words in French plural form.

Ample, multiple, simple, triple

1.C'est une fille naturelle, spontanée, sans manière, très…..

2. quatre est le ……..de deux

3. cette robe est large, elle est…….

4. il s'est trompé trois fois, c'est une ……erreur

:

84

Chapter 3- French and English nouns and adjectives that have the same pronunciation

a) Nouns in "age"

1.Camouflage

2.Corsage

3.Entourage

4.Maquillage

5.Reportage

6.Sabotage

.

b) Nouns in "arium and orium"

1.Aquarium

2.Auditorium

3.Crematorium

4.Planétarium

5. Solarium

Please use this helpful tool https://voicenotebook.com/prononce.php which allows you to check the similarity of pronunciation in English and French.

c) Nouns in -ence
1.Adolescence

2.Coexistence

3.Convalescence

4.Convergence

5.Magnificence

6.Opalescence

7.Réminiscence

Please use this helpful tool

https://voicenotebook.com/prononce.php

which allows you to check the similarity of pronunciation

in English and French.

d) Nouns in -ette

1. Barrette
2. cadette
3. cigarette
4. coquette
5. Etiquette
6. Kitchenette
7. Gazette
8. majorette
9. marionette
10. palette
11. silhouette
12. statuette
13. vignette

Please use this helpful tool https://voicenotebook.com/prononce.php

which allows you to check the similarity of pronunciation in English and French.

e) Adjectives in esque

1.   Arabesque
2.   Burlesque
3.   Grotesque
4.   Romanesque
5.   Statuesque

Please use this helpful tool https://voicenotebook.com/prononce.php which allows you to check   the similarity of pronunciation in English and French.

Correction exercizes

Exercize 1 :

1.   contacts
2.   Il manque de tact
3.   tracts
4.   artefacts
5.   **impact**

Exercize 2 :

1.   promenade
2.   grillades
3.   La tapenade
4.   fusillade
5.   oreangeade

Exercize 3 '

Age, voyages, image, message, pages

1. pages
2. message
3. voyages
4. âge
5. image

Exercize 4

Aquarium, auditorium, crématorium, planetarium, solarium

1. aquarium
2. solarium
3. planetarium
4. auditorium
5. crématorium

Exercize 5

<u>Complete the sentences using the following words in French :</u>

1. pesticides
2. génocide
3. homicide
4. insecticides
5. bactéricide

Exercize 6

<u>Complete the sentences using the following words in French :</u>

Absences, intelligence, sciences, violence, silence

1. sciences
2. intelligence
3. violence
4. silence
5. absent

Exercize 7

<u>Complete the sentences using the following words in French :</u>

1. Automobile
2. domicile
3. reptiles
4. piles
5. missile

Exercize 8

Complete the sentences using the following words in French :

Formation, location, relations, tradition, vocation

1.relations

2. location

3. tradition

4. formation

5. vocation

Exercize 9

Complete the sentences using the following words in French :

Vitamines, cuisine, piscine, routine, vitrines

1. vitrines
2. vitamines
3. cuisine
4. piscine
5. routine

Exercize 10

1. triple
2. temple
3. couple

Exercize 11

1. altitude
2. solitude
3. certitude
4. habitude
5. J'ai fait études

Exercize 12

1. vitale
2. normal
3. géniaux
4. principale
5. capital

Exercize 13

1. potable
2. portable
3. respectable
4. rechargeable
5. insatiable

Exercize 14

Complete the sentences using the following words in French :

Compact, exacte, intact

      1.   compact
      2.   exacte
      3.   intact

Exercize 15

      1.   innocent
      2.   effervescent
      3.   succulent
      4.   violent
      5.   excellent

Exercize 16

1.   convainquant
2.   important
3.   stimulant

Exercize 17

Grotesques, romanesque, burlesque, statuesque

1. grostseque
2. romanesque
3. burlesque
4. statuesque

Exercize 18

Complete the sentences using the following words in French :

Cordiale, familiaux, spéciaux, spatiale, sociale

1. familiaux
2. spatiale
3. spéciaux
4. cordiale
5. sociale

Exercize 19

Complete the sentences using the following words in French :

Exercize 20

Complete the sentences using the following words in French :

Accessible, compatibles, horrible, invicible, visible

1. horrible
2. accessible
3. compatibles
4. invincible
5. visible

Exercize 21

Complete the sentences using the following words in French

Déficient, impatient, inconscient, efficiente, patient

6. déficient
7. patient
8. impatient
9. Il inconscient
10. Efficiente

Exercize 22

Complete the sentences using the following words in French

Exercize 23

Complete the sentences using the following words in French

Fragile, hostile, mobile, virile, facile

1. fragile
2. virile
3. facile
4. mobile
5. hostile

Exercize 24

Complete the sentences using the following words in French

plural form.

Clandestine, divine, masculine, sanguines

1. clandestine
2. divine
3. masculine
4. sanguines

Exercize 25

Complete the sentences using the following words in French
plural form.
1. simple
2. multiple
3. ample
4. triple

Conclusion

I hope my book which is a learning tool to master French vocabulary will help you obtain a solid base in your knowledge of the French language. This 1000 +++ words contained in this edition will easily aid in your understanding of simple to complex phrases and hone your speaking and written skills. Simple analogies of each word in both languages will assist in the spontaneous memorization of the French word. Once you have browsed 90% of the words contained in my list, you will be able to say : "Yes ! I can see, I know French for ever which encourage me to speak, to read and write with the same native confidence I have always have.

For more information, please visit www.personalfrenchteacher.com .

If you have any question, suggestion or feedback, please contact us : info@personalfrenchteacher.com

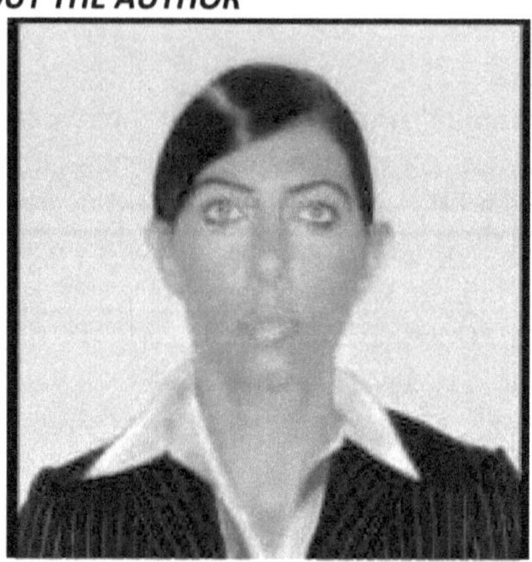

Catherine- Chantal Marango is a highly trained French multilingual professional who has many years of experience as a successful Foreign Language Expert, working in Nice, France.

She celebrates with her Mediterranean enthusiasm 10 years being in the Language business.

Successfully running her linguistic company Personal French Teacher (www.personalfrenchteacher.com), she has worked with thousands of high-qualified global students seeking a real language improvement from general to specific purposes.

Her real-world experience, multilingualism, multiculturalism, extensive education and pragmatic connection make her the excellent choice to help you speak the world with flying colors.

Now, by reading her books and taking her courses, it is your chance to be a real success, a five star language speaker for ever!!!